BOURBON MIXOLOGY

50 Bourbon Cocktails from 50 Iconic Bars

BY
STEVE AKLEY

Written and Published by:
Steve Akley

Published by S.A.P. Entertainment © 2015

ISBN: 978-0-9906060-5-5

To Bourbon Mixologists Everywhere:

Enjoy these iconic cocktails at home, but don't miss the opportunity to visit these establishments if you get the chance!

Seriously… seek them out.

Even if you have to go out of your way to do so. They are worth the trip!

Bourbon Mixology
50 Bourbon Cocktails from 50 Iconic Bars

Introduction by Steve Akley, Author

There is something special about visiting an iconic bar. The establishment often has a life of its own from which you seemingly can draw energy.

It's like it comes to life with the essence of every person whom has ever worked or visited and enjoyed themselves there. The history of the location. The passion of the entrepreneur. The creativity of the mixologists. The uniqueness of its customer base.

It's all there!

Then again, as much fun as going to a great bar is, sometimes you just want to sit at home… or, maybe, you are hosting a gathering of friends. You want that extra special cocktail to wow your guests or to simply sip and enjoy during a quiet evening.

This edition of **Bourbon Mixology** is designed to provide you with the tools to make the perfect cocktail at home. Fifty signature cocktails from fifty iconic bars. At your fingertips, you get an all access pass to recreate a piece of these fifty legendary locations right whenever, and wherever, you want.

So channel some of the experience of visiting these fantastic locations by mixing up one of their cocktails from the comfort of your own home!

Cheers!
Note: Cocktail is Windmill Lounge's Sensuous Summer Sipper/p. 112

Table of Contents

Bale of Hay Saloon

344 West Wallace
Virginia City, MT 59755
(406) 843-5700

baleofhaysaloon.com

Established
1863

Leadership
Kay & Gay Rossow (twin sisters)

Note: Bale of Hay Saloon is operated mid-May to mid-September

Tarantula Juice

Originally made in town during the gold mining days with bourbon, gun powder and tobacco juice. It killed about half the guys who drank it. Ours tastes much better, and hasn't killed anyone... yet!

Submitted by: Bale of Hay Saloon

Serve in a rocks glass:

- 1 ½ ounces Willies Distillery Big Horn Bourbon
- ¾ ounce sweet vermouth
- 2 small dashes Angostura Bitters
- Maraschino cherry
- Add bourbon, vermouth and bitters to a mixing glass of ice
- Stir and strain into a rocks glass
- Garnish with a maraschino cherry

Big Star

1531 N. Damen
Chicago, IL 60622

bigstarchicago.com

Established
2009

BIGSTAR

Tiger Eyes

Big Star opened with plans to be a quiet little whiskey forward taqueria. That lasted about two seconds. With our cheap beer flowing, bonded shots of the day and Chef Paul Kahan designed tacos taking their hold on our city, we've shifted. We're often busy, and getting conceptually interesting Manhattans out to guests isn't always easy... but, we do always try to push the possibilities of that drink, subbing in interesting amaros that allow for layers of taste to shine through even during peak busy times. Tiger Eyes is just that -- a touch herbal, slightly sweet but with a light dry finish.

Submitted by: Laurent Lebec, Beverage Manager

Serve in an old fashioned glass:
- 2 ounces Buffalo Trace Bourbon
- ½ ounce Amaro Ciociaro
- ¼ ounce Luxardo Maraschino Liqueur
- ¼ ounce dry vermouth
- Add a dash of Angostura to an old fashioned glass along with rest of ingredients
- Stir
- Strain onto fresh ice and top with wormwood bitters

Bourbons Bistro

2255 Frankfort Avenue
Louisville, KY 40206
(502) 894-8838

bourbonsbistro.com
welovebourbon@bourbonsbistro.com

Established
2005

Leadership
Jason Brauner, Co-Owner
John Morrison, Co-Owner

BOURBONS
BISTRO
EST. 05

Maple Bacon Old Fashioned

Submitted by: Created by Bourbons Bistro Bar Manager, Jeff Shaw. Submitted by Event Manager, Annie Harlow.

Serve in a rocks glass:
- 2-3 ounces Knob Creek Bourbon Maple Bourbon
- Orange
- Cherry
- Bitters
- Bacon Simple Syrup (see recipe below)
- In a rocks glass, muddle orange, cherry, bitters and bacon simple syrup
- Fill with bourbon and top with ice

Bacon Simple Syrup
- Combine: bacon fat, sugar and warm water
- Filter

Bourbon and Branch

501 Jones Street
San Francisco, CA 94102
(415) 346-1735

bourbonandbranch.com
host@bourbonandbranch.com

Established
2006

Leadership
Brian Sheehy, Co-Owner
Doug Dalton, Co-Owner
Greg West, General Manager

Frank Lloyd

Submitted by: Bourbon and Branch

Serve in a coupe:
- 2 ounces Buffalo Trace Bourbon
- ½ ounce pear liqueur
- 4 dashes Laphroaig Scotch
- 4 dashes Nocino Walnut Liqueur
- 2 dashes Old fashioned bitters
- Combine all ingredients in a mixing glass, add ice
- Stir for about 80 rotations
- Strain into a small cocktail glass
- Express lemon oils over top of the cocktail
- Discard peel or hang on side of glass

Bourbon House

144 Bourbon Street
New Orleans, LA 70130
(504) 522-0111

bourbonhouse.com
feedback@bourbonhouse.com

Established
2002

Leadership
Dickie Brennan's restaurant group

New Fashioned

Before opening Bourbon House, key members of the Dickie Brennan team ventured to Kentucky to do some hands-on research. While there, they talked with Fred Noe, great-grandson of Jim Beam about classic bourbon cocktails and ideas to update them. One idea was using different fruits. The group thought "Louisiana and the Gulf Coast has some of the best produce in the country, why not incorporate that into a classic bourbon cocktail?" Thus, the *New Fashioned* was born. Today, bartenders at Bourbon House use seasonal fruit – peaches, strawberries and blueberries to create this delicious cocktail.

Submitted by: Bourbon House

Serve in a rocks glass:
- 2 ounces macerated peaches (fruit marinated in its own juices with a touch of sugar overnight - blueberries, raspberries or strawberries may be substituted)
- 2 ounces Knob Creek Bourbon
- 5 shakes Peychaud's Bitters
- 1 splash simple syrup
- 1 splash soda
- Combine macerated fruit, bitters, splash of simple syrup and splash of soda in a rocks glass and muddle
- Add Knob Creek, fill with ice and mix well

Bub City
435 North Clark
Chicago, IL 60654
(312) 610-4200

bubcitychicago.com

Leadership
RJ Melman, Jerrod Melman, Molly Melman & Doug Psaltis

Bub City Old Fashioned

It's a great bourbon cocktail no matter the weather or season, and you can alter the flavor profile by changing up the bitters that you top the drink with.

Submitted by: Diane Corcoran, Beverage Director

Serve in a double old fashioned glass:
- 2 ½ ounces Very Old Barton Bourbon
- ¼ ounce Demerara Syrup
- 4 dashes Angostura Bitters
- Ice
- Orange peel and Luxardo cherry, for garnish
- 4 drops Bittercube Cherry Bark Vanilla Bitters, for garnish
- Combine bourbon, Demerara syrup and Angostura Bitters in a mixing glass; add ice and stir 30 seconds
- Strain into a double old fashioned glass over a large cube of ice
- Garnish with orange peel, Luxardo cherry and 4 drops Bittercube bitters

Buckhorn Exchange

1000 Osage Street
Denver, Colorado 80204
(303) 534-9505

buckhorn.com

Established
1893

Leadership
Christopher Murray, Beverage Manager

Buffalo Bill Cocktail

Buffalo Bill used to enjoy rye whiskey and hard apple cider so this is an update to his favorite cocktail.

Submitted by: Buckhorn Exchange

Serve in a highball glass:
- 1 ¼ ounces Bourbon
- 3 ounces Apple juice
- Serve over ice

Buffalo Bodega Gaming Complex

658 Main Street
Deadwood, SD 57783
(605) 578-1162

buffalobodega.com
kevin@kajhospitality.com

Established
1877

Leadership
Kevin Johnson

Buffalo Bodega Gaming Complex, formerly The Buffalo, was actually the NEWEST bar in town when it became the city's 18th saloon during the heyday of Buffalo Bill Cody, a close friend of original owner Mike Russell. Today, it is the oldest bar in South Dakota. You can still drink and gamble there (with considerably less risk of being shot) and even get a room at the Bullock Hotel upstairs.

The Keo

This is a simple drink, representing a late local of fame in Deadwood. If you know someone in Deadwood, chances are they have a Keo story to tell. This was his favorite bourbon!

Submitted by: Rob Lyons, Bar Manager

Serve in a tumbler:
- Shot of Buffalo Trace Bourbon
- Big rocks (ice)
- Cock 'n Bull Ginger Beer
- Lime
- Place your big rocks in a tumbler
- Pour the bourbon, wedge of lime and fill the glass with the ginger beer

Butter Run Saloon

27626 Harper Avenue
St Clair Shores, MI 48081
(586) 675-2115

butterrun.com

Established
2012

Leadership
David Harden

Basil Basil

Along the lines of an Old Fashioned (muddled cherry, sugar, bitters and bourbon), and also somewhat like a mint julep (mint, sugar and bourbon), the Basil Basil is a refreshing drink… perfect for a hot summer day.

Submitted by: Sonny Geha

Serve in an old fashioned or highball glass:
- 1 ½ ounces Basil Hayden
- ¼ ounce St. Germain (elderflower liqueur)
- 2 or 3 large fresh basil leaves (save one for garnish)
- 3 or 4 dashes of grapefruit bitters
- 1 sugar cube or a packet of sugar
- Add sugar, grapefruit bitters and basil (1 large leaf or 2 smaller leaves) to glass and muddle (preferably a muddler with teeth) until the mixture resembles a green paste
- Pour in Basil Hayden and St. Germain and then stir
- Add ice to fill the glass
- Transfer contents to shaker and shake vigorously only a few times, the idea is to dissolve the sugar and create a frothy drink, however, if you shake it too much, the ice will begin to melt and dilute the drink
- Pour contents of shaker back into glass (with ice) and garnish with basil leaf

Down One Bourbon Bar and Restaurant

321 West Main Street
Louisville, KY 40202
(502) 566-3259

downonebourbonbar.com
bburrows@downonebourbonbar.com

Established
2012

7 Across the Board

(Notes by Beth Burrows, the creator of this award-winning, Down One Bourbon Bar signature cocktail.) This cocktail was created for a Derby-themed, Bourbon Cocktail Competition in 2014. The sponsor was Angel's Envy and I was being rather sentimental about spring, thinking of the times that I used to pick blackberries and raspberries behind my grandmother's house in Western New York. I ran with the thought, and now had a base spirit and a flavor profile. I began cooking a simple syrup with raspberries. I soon realized that it needed an herb to round it out. Tradition says mint for Derby, and although this was for a Derby competition, I wanted to create a cocktail that wasn't pigeon-holed into any one season. I went to the store and grabbed some sage, tarragon, and rosemary. I tried making a simple syrup with each of the three - sage won, hands down. Next the blackberry was pureed and strained into a seedless, liquid form. The cocktail was good, but it was a bit tart and too sweet. It needed more; and I still had no Derby tie in. My general manager, Christian Hattemer and I had been looking into smoking cocktails, so we gave it a try. It was makeshift at first, routing out an oak plank to fit a glass, and quartino, but we made it work!

Now, for a Derby theme. As Christian and I are discussing the cocktail, there was a regular customer drinking and listening. Christian asked, "When you think Derby, what comes to mind?" "Horses, of course," I replied. "What about Horses?" he asked. Instinctively I said "Hay is for horses," which is a smart-aleck quip I learned from my mother at a young age. (It was often her response when I would give a disgruntled "Heeeeyyyyy" in reference to whatever was 'offending' me at the time.) "Where would I even get hay from," I asked. Right about then, that regular of mine said that he just so happens to deliver hay to Churchill Downs regularly and if I was interested, a bundle was mine. I enthusiastically agreed, but didn't know if it would really come together. The next day, I had a bundle of hay waiting for me behind the bar. I went to the competition without a name for the cocktail, hoping to wing it. In the registration paperwork I had to list a name. At a loss, I did what I do at Churchill when I can't decide on a bet: I wrote "7 Across the Board." The cocktail won the competition....and the rest is history.

Submitted by: Beth Burrows, Assistant General Manager

Serve in a large rocks glass:
- 2 ounces Angel's Envy Bourbon
- 1 ounce raspberry sage simple
- 1 ounce blackberry puree
- Combine and shake with ice
- Strain into quartino glass and top with small ice ball
- Smoke a (used) bourbon barrel oak stave until flame forms
- Toss a bundle of Timothy Hay (from Churchill Downs) onto the flame and smother with a large rocks glass
- Let the glass smoke for a little bit of time, then turn up the glass and allow the smoke to escape
- Turn the quartino over and let the ice ball gently fall into the glass, followed by the cocktail

E. Smith Mercantile

208 1st Avenue South
Seattle, WA 98104
(206) 641-7250

esmithmercantile.com
info@esmithmercantile.com

Established
2013

Leadership
Kate, Jesse and Sara Poole

Cure-All

We approach the art of cocktail crafting with a medicinal focus. Early uses for alcohol were to administer medicine by extracting plant essences, and let's be honest, calming the nerves and reducing pain. The horehound herb has traditionally been used to treat respiratory ailments, so our Cure-All cocktail is an excellent selection during cold and flu season and to beat off pesky allergies.

Submitted by: Bartender Jessie

Serve in a rocks glass:

- 1 ½ ounces Horehound (a bitter herb) infused bourbon
- ½ ounce bourbon
- ¾ ounce cherry heering
- 1 oz fresh squeezed orange juice
- Pour all ingredients in a shaker, add ice and shake to a crema (foam)
- Serve in a rocks glass with shaken (broken) ice
- Garnish with an orange twist, twisting the peel over the cocktail

El Gaucho

2505 1st Avenue
Seattle, WA 98121
(206) 728-1337

elgaucho.com
info@elgaucho.com

Leadership
El Gaucho Hospitality Group

El Gaucho Hickory Manhattan

(Notes by James Capangpangan, General Manager, El Gaucho Tacoma) El Gaucho has a legacy of old-school tableside service. Caesar salads, flaming tenderloin brochettes and Bananas Foster are part of our tradition. We like to add new tableside preparations every so often and the team at El Gaucho Tacoma took the challenge to create something which encompasses both visual appeal and aromatic senses. After brainstorming some ideas on food with the whole management team, Bartender Joe Vego had suggested we do a drink to tie in the full start to finish table side experience.

The smoking tableside idea only seemed natural to do it with bourbon, since bourbon can take on so many different flavors. We originally wanted to smoke the drink with bourbon soaked oak barrel wood chips, but those chips were not going to be delivered fast enough, so we ran to a local grocery store and picked up hickory chips just so we can start testing out our presentation. The hickory made the Manhattan taste so good, that we decided to stick with it.

We started off with trying to smoke a finished Eagle Rare 10 year Manhattan, made with Carpano's Antica Formula sweet vermouth and a couple dashes of bitters in a rocks glass, but that produced too much smoke and made the dining room seem cloudy. Also, the show didn't look too great because it was so dark in the restaurant. That's when the beverage transitioned to smoke washing the glass instead of fully smoking the Manhattan. Still, we were running into a presentation problem because we have a dimly lit restaurant. I remember talking about this problem with my wife and my 11-year-old daughter overheard our conversation and suggested that we use the new ice sphere that I have been raving about. I kind of shrugged it off at the time and the next night of testing Jacob our wine captain also suggested the same thing!

We bought some LED base lights to up-light the smoke show of the glass, we form a crystal clear ice sphere from Creative Ice as the glass is getting smoke washed and combine everything at the end garnishing it with brandy soaked Griottes cherries!

That is how The Hickory Manhattan was born!

Submitted by: James Capangpangan, General Manager

Serve in a bucket glass:
- 2 ounces Eagle Rare 10 Year Bourbon
- 1 ounces Carpano Antica Formula Vermouth
- 3 dashes Angostura Bitters
- 3 Griotte Brandy Soaked Cherries
- 1 orange peel, torched
- 1 oz hickory chips, torched
- Combine the bourbon, vermouth and bitters in a cocktail shaker with ice, shake to combine
- In a small bowl, add 1 ounce of hickory chips with 1 single orange peel laid over the hickory chips
- Torch with a butane lighter until contents are slightly burnt and will stay lit after the torch is taken away
- Allow to burn for about 5-10 seconds and then cup with a large bucket glass
- Allow smoke to wash the glass for about 30 seconds and then flip over to pour bourbon, vermouth, and bitters into glass over a large ice cube
- Garnish with the burnt orange peel and 3 brandy soaked Griotte cherries on a prism pick

El Moro Spirts & Tavern

945 Main Avenue
Durango, CO 81302
(970) 259-5555

elmorotavern.com
dave@elmorotavern.com

Established
2013 (on the site of the El Moro Tavern, a 1900s era saloon)

Leadership
Dave Woodruff, General Manager
Lucas Hess, Assistant General Manager

Sheriff's Daisy

(Notes by Lucas Hess): I came up with this cocktail for our summer cocktail menu and it has been a top seller since it was released. This was his riff on a classic daisy cocktail utilizing bourbon to shine. The "Sheriff" part of the name comes from the history of the bar in that the sheriff in 1906 (Bill Thompson) was shot and killed in our establishment by the town marshal (Jesse Stansel).

Submitted by: Lucas Hess

Serve in a rocks glass:
- 1 ½ ounces Old Forester Bourbon
- ¼ ounce yellow chartreuse
- ¾ ounce lime juice
- ½ ounce agave simple syrup (recipe below)
- Pour all ingredients into a shaker and add ice and shake until well blended and cold
- Double strain into an 8 ounce rocks glass
- Add ice and garnish with mint sprig

Agave Simple Syrup Recipe
- 23 ounces store-bought agave syrup
- 23 ounces water
- 1 tablespoon whole coriander
- 13 whole peppercorns
- Peel from half an orange
- Combine all ingredients into a medium sized saucepan over medium heat

Agave Simple Syrup Recipe (continued)

- Heat until just boiling while stirring occasionally
- Reduce heat to low and allow to simmer for 8 minutes
- Strain solids out of liquid and refrigerate (Should last 2-3 weeks)

Equus and Jack's Lounge

122 Sears Avenue
Louisville, KY 4007
(502) 897-9721

equusrestaurant.com
arnett.equus@gmail.com

Established
1985

Leadership
Ryan Arnett, General Manager

Bourbon Ball

The Bourbon Ball is the signature bourbon cocktail at Equus and Jack's Lounge. It was crafted by Joy Perrine who co-authored the ***Kentucky Bourbon Cocktail Book***. Not only is Joy writing books, and crafting unique cocktails at Equus and Jack's, she hosts her own event at the yearly Bourbon Festival in Bardstown, Kentucky.

Submitted by: Joy Perrine

Serve in a rocks glass:
- Equal parts Woodford Reserve Bourbon, Tuaca and Dekuyper Dark Crème de Cocoa
- Shake ingredients over ice
- Strain into a rocks glass
- Garnish with a cherry

The Esquire Tavern

155 East Commerce Street
San Antonio, TX 78205
(210) 222-2521

esquiretavern-sa.com
info@esquiretavern-sa.com

Established
1933

Leadership
Christopher Hill, Proprietor
Garry Baker, General Manager
Houston Eaves, Beverage Director
Brooke Smith, Executive Chef
Myles Worrell, Bar Manager
Justin Solomon, Director of Operations

Wonderlust King

This Manhattan-inspired cocktail was created by Bar Manager Myles Worrell in 2014, to present to King Cocktail, Dale Degroff. Named for the Gogol Bordello song of the same name.

Submitted by: Myles Worrell

Serve in a coupe:

- 2 ounces Old Fitzgerald Bottled in Bond Bourbon
- ¾ ounce Cocchi di Torino
- ½ ounce Nardini Amaro
- 1 dash Bittermen's Xocolate Mole Bitters
- 1 dash Regan's Orange Bitters
- Orange peel
- Combine ingredients in mixing glass with ice
- Stir well
- Strain into chilled coupe
- Express orange oil over cocktail
- Trim zest into fanciful bird and place on glass

FAR BAR

347 East 1st Street
Los Angeles, CA 90012
(213) 617-9990

farbarla.com
farbarla@gmail.com

Established
2006

Leadership
Mike Gin, Co-Owner
Don Tahara, Co-Owner
George Kleven, General Manager
Sean Naughton, Bar Director

Kung-Fu Buffalo

At Far Bar, we feature one of the largest whiskey and bourbon selections in Downtown Los Angeles. We love to find ways of incorporating Japanese ingredients into our whiskey cocktails. In this case, we are featuring the always versatile Buffalo Trace Bourbon with fresh Yuzu juice. The vanilla and the maraschino liqueurs highlight some of Buffalo Trace's dominant flavors and balance the tartness of the yuzu. The egg white was an afterthought, but once we went there, it gave the cocktail a delicious meringue that pulled the whole idea together.

Submitted by: Sean Naughton, Bar Director

Serve in a coupe:
- 1 ½ ounces Buffalo Trace Bourbon
- ¾ ounce fresh yuzu juice
- ½ ounce Liqueur 43
- ½ ounce Luxardo Maraschino Liqueur
- 1 egg white
- Peychaud's Bitters
- Put all ingredients in a shaker tin and dry shake
- Add ice and shake vigorously
- Strain into a coupe glass
- Garnish with a few dashes of Peychaud's Bitters

Forbidden Island Tiki Lounge

1304 Lincoln Avenue
Alameda, CA 94501
(510) 749-0332

forbiddenislandalameda.com
info@forbiddenislandalameda.com

Established
2006

Leadership
Michael and Mano Thanos

Vic Valentine

The Vic Valentine was originally featured as part of a special menu available on monthly film nights called "Forbidden Thrills," programmed and hosted by local B movie impresario/pulp fiction author, Will "the Thrill" Viharo. Named after the private eye protagonist of Viharo's pulp fiction novels, Vic Valentine accents the noir flavor of bourbon with jazzy notes of cherry, lemon, cinnamon and vanilla.

Submitted by: Former General Manager Sue Eggett

Serve in a double rocks glass:

- 1 ½ ounces Jim Beam Bourbon
- 1 ounce lemon juice
- ½ ounce cinnamon vanilla syrup
- ½ ounce cherry heering
- ¼ ounce Luxardo Maraschino Liqueur
- Shake ingredients together and serve with ice, garnished with a long lemon zest

Gallagher's Restaurant
114 W. Mill Street
Waterloo, IL 62298
(618) 939-9933

gallagherswaterloo.com

Established
2003

Leadership
John and Susie Gallagher, Owners

Classic Whiskey Sour

Submitted by: James Gallagher

Serve in a rocks glass:
- 1 ½ oounces Buffalo Trace Bourbon
- 1 egg white
- Juice from half a lemon
- 1 ounce dark simple syrup (brown sugar based)
- 3 shakes Regans Orange Bitters
- 1 shake Angostura Bitters
- Luxardo cherry and juice
- Orange wheel (garnish)
- Pour Buffalo Trace in an old fashioned glass filled with ice
- Garnish with orange slice
- Crack egg and juggle yolk between shell halves to separate white from yolk
- Place egg white in a martini shaker and discard yolk
- Add juice of half a lemon
- Add 1 ounce of dark simple syrup (If you have to make syrup - combine equal parts brown sugar and water and heat on stove until all sugar dissolves)
- Add both bitters
- Shake very vigorously without ice to emulsify egg and turn mixture into a frothy white foam
- Strain on top of whiskey and ice which will create a layer that resembles a head for beer
- Top with 1 Luxardo cherry and drizzle a small amount of cherry juice onto of the frothy head to create a fantastic presentation

Hard Water

Pier 3 The Embarcadero
San Francisco, CA 94105
(415) 392-3021

hardwaterbar.com
info@hardwaterbar.com

Leadership
The Slanted Door Group

Bourbon Lift

Long time Slanted Door bartender and owner of Small Hand Foods, Jennifer Colliau, had to do a drink for a competition with Benedictine. She wanted to lighten up the classic New Orleans Brandy Milk Punch with soda water. It turns out that she made an alcoholic New York egg cream. We bantered around with some names and settled on "Lift." It seemed to fit with the fixes, fizzes, toddys, etc.

When Hard Water opened, we did a bourbon version of the Lift. It kind of has the texture of a root beer float. The bubbles from the soda water are present in the head. We serve the drink with a small spoon straw so that the guests can eat the foam. The drink is both calorically heavy and light and airy.

Submitted by: Hard Water (created by Jennifer Colliau)

Serve in a fizz glass:
- 1 ½ ounce Buffalo Trace Bourbon
- ½ ounce Small Hand Foods Orgeat (available online)
- ½ ounce organic straus cream
- ½ ounce St. George NOLA Coffee Liqueur
- Soda water (Q brand is suggested)
- Shake everything except soda water and strain into an 8 ounce fizz glass
- Add soda water to fill the glass
- Stir the drink (paddle back and forth) while adding the soda to achieve a good head
- After it sits for 20 seconds, or so, add an ounce more soda water to "lift" the head above the glass
- Serve with metal spoon straw

Herbie's Vintage 72

405 N. Euclid
St. Louis, MO 63108
(314) 769-9595

herbies.com
amanda@herbies.com

Established
2008

Leadership
Aaron Teitelbaum, owner

In Fashion

(Notes by Amanda Wilgus.) The In Fashion was inspired by the classic cocktail the Old Fashioned. An old fashioned is traditionally made with a sugar cube, Angostora Bitters, 1 cherry, 1 orange and bourbon. I replaced the sugar cube with simple syrup, the cherry with the Luxardo Maraschino Liqueur, the orange with the kumqaut and the Angostora with blood orange bitters. The result is something that's a little more approachable and lighter for the warm summer months.

Submitted by: Amanda Wilgus, Bar Manager

Serve in a double rocks glass:

- ½ ounce Luxardo Maraschino Liqueur
- ½ ounce Simple syrup
- 2 ounce Buffalo Trace Bourbon
- 1 kumquat
- 1 capful Stirrings Blood Orange Bitters
- Muddle kumquat and simple syrup
- Add bourbon, cherry liqueur, bitters and stir
- Pour all ingredient into a double rocks glass and top with fresh ice if needed

Jack Rose Dining Saloon

2007 18th Street NW
Washington, DC 20009
(202) 588-7388

jackrosediningsaloon.com

Established
2011

Leadership
Bill Thomas, Co-Owner
Steve King, Co-Owner

Lemonade Parade

Submitted by: Trevor Frye, Beverage Director

Serve in a tulip glass:
- 1 ¼ ounce Baker's Bourbon
- ½ ounce Jack Rose house tonic (recipe below)
- ¼ ounce lemon
- ¼ ounce honey
- 1 dash Fee Brothers Whiskey Barrel Aged Bitters
- Combine all ingredients into a cocktail shaker
- Add ice, shake and strain into an iced tulip glass
- Top with soda and garnish with lemon balm leaf

Jack Rose House Tonic Recipe
- 2 ¼ cups water
- 2 ⅓ cups dried cut lemon grass
- Zest of 2 lemons and limes
- 11 grams of gentian
- 1 gram of wormword
- 1 ¼ teaspoons citric acid
- ¼ teaspoon black pepper kernels
- Bring all ingredients to a boil and then lower to simmer for 45 minutes
- Remove from heat and allow to steep for 20 minutes
- Fine strain through a cheese cloth onto 2 cups of sugar
- Let cool before using in cocktail

The Lovecraft Bar

421 SE Grand Avenue
Portland, OR 97217

thelovecraftbar.com
lovecraftcontact@gmail.com

Established
2011

Leadership
Jon Horrid

Argento

Submitted by: Brook Moreno

 or

Serve in a collins (iced) or Irish coffee (hot) glass:
- 1 shot Buffalo Trace Bourbon
- ½ shot Di Saronno Amaretto
- Top off with Jasmine Pearl Amaretto Spiced Tea and a splash of sour
- Garnish with a lemon wedge
- Can be served iced or hot

Tea Instructions

Brewing (8 ounce serving)
- Scoop a slightly heaping teaspoon of tea leaves into your infuser
- Heat water to 190 degrees (just before boiling)
- Pour 8 ounces of water over tea leaves
- Steep tea for 3-5 minutes (depending on taste preference)
- Remove infuser and add to cocktail

Iced Tea
Our opinion is that a cooled concentrate works best, as regular-strength brew tends to become watery as the ice melts. So, use the above leaf quantities, but half the water, allow it to cool, then mix it into your cocktail. The brew will dilute down to proper strength as the ice melts.

Martin's Tavern

1264 Wisconsin Avenue, NW
Washington, D.C. 20007
(202) 333-7370

martinstavern.com

Established
1933

Leadership
William A. Martin, Jr. (fourth generation owner)

Martin's Tavern has had the honor of serving every President from Harry S. Truman (Booth 6) to George W. Bush (Table 12). Many had their favorite booths and would visit frequently. In fact, John F. Kennedy proposed to Jacqueline Bouvier in Booth #3… now known as the "Kennedy Booth" or "The Proposal Booth."

Harry S Truman's Daily Ritual

Martin's Tavern would like to tie our recipe into our history - the connections to the U.S. Presidents and the Martin family. As a Congressman, then Senator from Missouri, and then as Vice President, Harry Truman sat in Booth 6 with colleagues at Martin's Tavern. In the fall of 1942 his daughter Margaret entered George Washington University and Truman dined in Booth 6 in Martin's with Margaret and his wife Bess.

Submitted by: Chrissy Gardner, Martin's Tavern

Serve in a shot glass:
- Rise early and take a one or two mile brisk walk
- Have a rubdown
- Take a shot of Virginia Gentleman Bourbon
- Enjoy a light breakfast
- Go to the office (in his case the Oval Office) to start your day

Mike Shannon's Steaks and Seafood

620 Market Street
St. Louis MO 63101
(314) 421-1540

shannonsteak.com
info@shannonsteak.com

Established
1985

Leadership
Mike and Patricia Shannon

SAINT LOUIS

STEAKS AND SEAFOOD

The Doc Watson

Submitted by: Mike Shannon's Steaks and Seafood

Serve in a rocks glass:
- 1 ½ ounces Hatfield & McCoy Bourbon
- ¾ ounce Solerno Blood Orange Liqueur
- ½ ounce cane syrup
- ½ ounce fresh squeezed lemon juice,
- 2 dashes rhubarb bitters
- Shake all well and serve in rocks glass with garnish of a smoked orange rind

Miller House

301 East 5th Street
Owensboro, KY 42303
(270) 685-5878

themillerhouserestaurant.com

Established
2009

Leadership
Larry & Jeanne Kirk, Owners

Southern Lady Martini

Submitted by: The Miller House

Serve in a martini glass:
- 1 ½ ounces Wathen's Bourbon
- ¼ ounce Peach Schnapps
- 2 ounce house made peach mix (recipe below)
- Garnish with a peach wedge and mint

House Made Peach Mix
- 24 ounce concentrated peach nectar
- 5 tablespoons peach compound
- Whisk together in a pitcher

Mongoose versus Cobra

1011 Mcgowen
Houston, TX 77004
(713) 650-6872

mongooseversuscobra.com
info@mongooseversuscobra.com

Established
2012

Leadership
Ian Rosenberg, Owner
Mike Sammons, Owner
Corey Walton, Manager

Gold Rush #2

Submitted by: Mongoose versus Cobra

Serve in a rocks glass:
- 2 ounces bourbon
- 1 ounce honey rosemary syrup
- ¾ ounce lemon juice
- Shake and strain over ice
- Top with soda
- Garnish with rosemary and lemon

9th Street Public House

36 N 9th Street
Columbia, MO 65201

9thstreetpublichouse.com

Established
2014

Leadership
James Kanne, Owner
Michael De Leon, Bar Manager

Show-Me Manhattan

Submitted by: Michael De Leon

Serve in a chilled stemless martini glass:
- 2 ½ ounces J. Rieger's and Co. Kansas City Bourbon
- 1 ounce Carpano Antica Sweet Red Vermouth
- ½ ounce Punt e Mes Vermouth
- 2-3 Dashes Dale Degroffs Pimento Bitters
- Thick lemon twist for garnish
- Luxardo cherry
- Chill a stemless Martini glass in the freezer for 30-45 seconds
- Meanwhile, fill a glass half with ice
- Add bourbon, vermouths, and bitters
- Stir for around 60 seconds, making sure to stir the ice and liquid around the glass not stirring the bar spoon around the ice and liquid... just enough to chill
- Strain into the chill stemless martini glass
- Slice a fresh thick slice of lemon rind and squeeze over the Manhattan releasing oils
- Drop in a Luxardo cherry and enjoy

Old Ebbitt Grill

675 15th St NW
Washington, DC 20005
(202) 347-4800

oldebbitt.com

Established
1856

Leadership
Clyde's Restaurant Group

Michter's Manhattan

Submitted by: Old Ebbitt Grill

Serve in a bird bath:
- 2 ounces Michter's Single Barrel Bourbon
- 1 ounce Sweet Vermouth
- 2 dashes Angostura Bitters
- Mix ingredients into cocktail shaker with ice, shake well and strain into chilled bird bath
- Garnish with a cherry and serve

Old Major

3316 Tejon
Denver, CO 80211

oldmajor.com

Established
2013

Leadership
Justin Brunson, Owner

Modern Savage
Named after Patrick Swayze's character in *Point Break*.

Submitted by: Michael McGill, Bar Manager at Old Major

Serve in a double rocks glass:
- ½ ounce Buffalo Trace Bourbon
- ¾ ounce Amaro Nonino
- ¾ ounce Cocchi Torino Vermouth
- 2 large dashes of root beer bitters
- Stir in double old fashioned glass over a large ice cube
- Garnish with an orange peel

Parlay Social

249 W. Short Street
Lexington, KY 40507
(859) 244-1932

parlaysocial.com

Established
2011

Leadership
Bob Estes, Owner
Oliver Winn, Bar Manager

Smoked Manhattan

Submitted by: Oliver Winn

Serve in a chilled martini glass:
- 1 ½ ounces Makers 46 Bourbon
- ½ ounce Dollini Sweet Vermouth
- 5 dashes of smoked orange bitters (a cocktail punk may be used to smoke bitters)
- 1 oak stave (preferably a Makers 46 stave)
- Place fresh oak stave in a cast iron skillet and use a blowtorch to char the stave
- Once charred, place your chilled martini glass over the stave to capture the smoke
- Let set for 5 to 10 seconds allowing the smoke to meld with the glass
- Remove and pour all ingredients in glass add a bourbon soaked cherry and it is ready to be served

Parson's Chicken and Fish

2952 W Armitage Avenue
Chicago, IL 60647
(773) 384-3333

parsonschickenandfish.com
info@parsonschickenandfish.com

Leadership
Owned by Land and Sea Dept.

Darkness

This one is a banger!

Submitted by: Charlie Schott, Parson's Chicken and Fish

Serve in a rocks glass:

- 1 ¼ ounces Old Grandad 100 proof Bourbon
- ½ ounce Averna
- ¼ ounce Fernet Branca
- ¼ ounce Cruzan Blackstrap Rum
- 1 bar spoon cinnamon simple syrup (recipe below)
- 2 dashes Angostura Bitters
- Stir in all ingredients and serve over ice in a rocks glass expressed with lemon oil with no garnish

Cinnamon Simple Syrup

- ½ cup sugar water
- 4 cinnamon sticks
- Simmer for 15 minutes
- Strain

Peacock Alley

422 E. Main Avenue
Bismarck, ND 58501
(701) 221-BEEF (2333)

peacock-alley.com
peacockalleycrew@gmail.com

Established
1933

Leadership
Dale and Melodie Zimmerman

Downtown Bruiser

The name came from a customer who frequents the Peacock Alley. He looks like a bruiser because of his size but likes all kinds of drinks, even sweet ones. We came up with the drink using some old ingredients like Fernet Branca, but wanted to add an ingredient that was currently very hot. This is why we added ginger beer. We wanted to make a drink that would be approachable to new bourbon drinkers. The bold aftertaste of Makers Mark is minimalized in the drink.

Submitted by: Dale Zimmerman

Serve in a cocktail glass:

- Fill glass with ice
- Pour 1.5 ounces Makers Mark Bourbon into the glass
- Add ½ ounce Fernet Branca
- Stir ingredients together
- Fill ¾ full with ginger beer

The Pope House Bourbon Lounge

2075 NW Glisan Street
Portland, OR 97209
(503) 222-1056

popehouselounge.com
info@popehouselounge.com

Established
2009

Leadership
Joel Carson, Owner
Kitling Lum, Owner
Miles Kusch, Owner

The Dalton

The beauty of this drink is that the coffee will melt and its flavor will get stronger as you drink it. The bitterness of the coffee is a nice counter point to the sweetness and richness of the cocktail. The brown sugar with the walnut bitters and bourbon give deep rich flavor.

Submitted by: Miles Kusch, The Pope House Bourbon Lounge

Serve in a large tumbler:

- 2 oz bourbon
- 1 teaspoon brown sugar
- 2 dashes black walnut bitters
- 1 large cube of frozen coffee
- One day ahead of time, freeze coffee in a 2" x 2" silicone mold
- Muddle brown sugar and walnut bitters
- Add bourbon
- Stir with ice and strain over coffee cube

The Porthole Restaurant and Pub

20 Custom House Wharf
Portland, ME 04101
(207) 773-4653

portholemaine.com
beth@casablancamaine.com

Established
1929

MacDonald's Mojito

Submitted by: Andrew MacDonald, The Porthole

Serve in a rocks glass:
- 1¾ ounces bourbon
- 4 ounces soda
- 1 strawberry (cut into fourths)
- Blackberries
- Basil leaf
- Lime
- Splash of simple syrup
- Muddle strawberry, blackberries and basil
- Add ice in glass, simple syrup, bourbon & soda
- Shake well & garnish with a lime

Downeast Honey B.
Bonus quick recipe. Hey, they had room in their chapter!

Submitted by: The Porthole Restaurant and Pub

Serve in a 10 oz cider glass:
- Pack glass with ice
- 1 ¼ ounces Bulleit Rye Bourbon
- Dash of bitters
- Top off glass with Downeast Honey Cider

Red Moon

234 Delaware Avenue
Put-in-Bay, OH 43456
(419) 285-2323

redmoonbar.com

Established
2015

Leadership
Paula Garsteck, General Manager

Tucked away in the Park Hotel, which was built in the 1870s, Red Moon is a true speakeasy.

Victory

Submitted by: Red Moon

Serve in a rocks glass:
- 1 ¼ ounces Woodford Reserve Bourbon
- ¾ ounce Chianti
- ½ ounce agave nectar
- ½ ounce passion fruit puree
- Mix all ingredients together in a rocks glass and garnish with an orange twist

The Roosevelt

623 North 25th Street
Richmond, VA 23223
(804) 658-1935

rooseveltrva.com
info@rooseveltrva.com

Established
2011

Leadership
Kendra Feather, Owner
Lee Gregory, Chef/Owner

Providence and Grace

Submitted by: Thomas Leggett, Bar Manager

Serve in a coupe:
- 1 ½ ounces Four Roses Bourbon
- ¾ ounce cream sherry
- ½ ounce Punt e Mes Italian Vermouth
- ½ ounce fresh lemon juice
- Dash Angostura Bitters
- Combine all ingredients and shake with ice
- Strain into chilled cocktail coupe and garnish with a lemon twist

The Round Robin Bar at Intercontinental The Willard

1401 Pennsylvania Ave NW
Washington, DC 20004
(202) 628-9100

washington.intercontinental.com

Established
1850

Henry Clay's Kentucky-Style Mint Julep

(As interpreted by Round Robin bartender Jim Hewes)
U.S. Senator Henry Clay of Kentucky introduced the drink to Washington, D.C., at the Round Robin Bar in the famous Willard Hotel during his residence in the city. The term "julep" is generally defined as a sweet drink, particularly one used as a vehicle for medicine. The word itself is derived from the Persian word گلاب (Golâb), meaning rose water.

Submitted by: Jim Hewes – Head Bartender Round Robin

Serve in a julep cup:

- 2 ounces Maker's Mark Bourbon
- 2 ounces San Pellegrino sparkling water
- 8-10 fresh mint leaves, plus a sprig of mint for garnish (Hewes uses red-stem mint)
- 2 cups crushed ice (dry, not slushy)
- 1 teaspoon granulated sugar plus a bit more to taste
- 1 thin strip lemon peel
- 1 julep cup (crystal or silver), frosted in the freezer
- 1 straw
- Add sugar, the mint leaves, one ounce bourbon, and one ounce sparkling water to the julep cup
- Using the heel of a butter knife, muddle for about a minute until it forms a tea
- Add a half cup of crushed ice and muddle some more
- Add the rest of the ice, keeping it tightly packed
- Pour in the rest of the bourbon and sparkling water
- Garnish with a sprig of mint and top with the lemon peel and a dusting of sugar
- Wedge the straw just behind the mint sprig so when you lean in for a sip, you get a peppery whiff

Sable Kitchen & Bar

505 North State Street
Chicago, IL 60654
(312) 755-9704

sablechicago.com
info@sablechicago.com

Leadership
Kimpton Hotels and Restaurants

Kentucky Grazer

The cocktail is essentially a riff on a bourbon smash but with pimms and celery bitters lending some additional savory and herbal elements to the flavor profile. The drink has great flavor complexity, is refreshing, but fairly simple to make.

Submitted by: Sable Kitchen & Bar

Serve in a rocks glass:

- 1 ½ ounces Buffalo Trace Bourbon
- ½ ounce fresh lemon juice
- ½ ounce Pimms
- ½ ounce simple syrup
- Mint sprig
- 1 heavy dash Bitter Truth Celery Bitters
- Combine all ingredients, shake and fine strain
- Serve in rocks glass over ice
- Garnish with mint sprig

Sanctuaria Wild Tapas

4198 Manchester Avenue
St. Louis, MO 63110
(314) 535-9700

sanctuariastl.com
wild@sanctuariastl.com

Established
2010

Clermont Confusion

Submitted by: Daniel Parker

Serve in a cocktail glass:
- 1 ½ ounces Sanctuaria Knob Creek Single Barrel Reserve
- ¾ ounce Dubonnet Rouge
- ¾ ounce Cynar
- ½ ounce Cointreau
- ½ ounce Pommeau
- ½ ounce creme de cacao
- Place all ingredients in a mixing glass and stir with a bar spoon
- Garnish with a flamed orange peel

Seviche, A Latin Restaurant

1538 Bardstown Road
Louisville KY 40205
(502) 473-8560

sevicherestaurant.com
sevicherestaurant@gmail.com

Established
2005

Superhorse

(Notes by Chris Derome.) I thought Superhorse was a good name for a rock-n-roll band. I imagine their sound being fast-tempo, but elegant, clean, high-pitched like a tenor, and with a good flow. That's just how this cocktail drinks.

Submitted by: Chris Derome, Bar Manager

Serve in a highball glass:
- 1.7 ounces Maker's Mark
- 1 ounce Domaine Canton ginger liquor
- ½ lemon
- ½ oz soda
- 5 drops sour orange bitters
- Combine Maker's, Domaine, lemon and soda in a dry shaker
- Hand stir
- Pour over ice and top with sour orange bitters

Sloppy Joe's

201 Duval Street
Key West, FL 33040
(305) 294-5715

sloppyjoes.com

Established
Located at the Corner of Duval and Greene Since 1937

Leadership
Chris Mullins, CEO

Sloppy Joe's Papa's Poison

Submitted by: Sloppy Joe's staff

Serve in a cocktail glass:
- 1 ½ ounces bourbon
- Top with ginger beer
- Squeeze of lemon
- Use a 12 ounce cup

Snow & Co.

1815 Wyandotte Street
Kansas City, MO 64108
(816) 214-8921

snowandcompany.com
info@snowandcompany.com

Established
2011

Leadership
Jerry Nevins, Co-Owner
Lauren Cloud, Co-Owner
Andy Talbert, Co-Owner

Miss Scarlett

This cocktail is created "granite-style" instead of in a blender.

Submitted by: Snow & Co.

Serve in a stylized glass with a straw:
- 3 ounces Stirrings Peach Liqueur
- 2 ounces Bulleit Bourbon
- 2 ounces whole milk
- 3 ounces simple syrup
- 3 ounces fresh lemon juice
- 2 ounces water
- Using a metal bowl, place in freezer and stir every 10-15 minutes until slushy in consistency
- Can also be frozen using an ice cream or gelato machine

St. Charles Exchange

113 South 7th Street
Louisville, KY 40202
(502) 618-1917

stcharlesexchange.com
lauren.farrar@stcharlesexchange.com

Established
2012

Leadership
Rob Frey and Amy Hoffmann Frey

Paper Trail

Submitted by: Colin Shearn

Serve in a Nick and Nora glass:
- 1 ¼ ounces Buffalo Trace Bourbon
- 1 ounce Aperol
- ¾ ounce Salers Syrup
- Stir over ice
- Garnish with a twist of grapefruit

The Sugar House

2130 Michigan Avenue
Detroit, MI 48216
(313) 962-0123

sugarhousedetroit.com
info@sugarhousedetroit.com

Established
2011

Leadership
Dave Kwiatkowski, Owner

EFK

A Sugar House original Old Fashioned using a culinary smoker to give the cocktail a charred wood, campfire-esque flavor.

Submitted by: The Sugar House

Serve in a rocks glass:
- 2 ounces Lapsang souchong infused Evan Williams Bourbon
- ½ ounce lemon simple syrup
- 3 dashes Angostura Bitters
- Stir and then smoked using hickory wood smoke captured from a culinary smoker
- Serve from bottle in a rocks glass over a hand carved 2" ice cube
- Express a lemon peel over rim and place in drink

Talbott Tavern

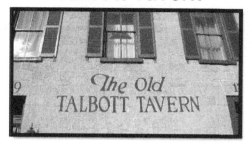

107 W. Stephen Foster Avenue
Bardstown, KY 40004
(502) 348-3494

talbotts.com
talbott@bardstown.com

Established
1779

"We are the original bourbon bar. We have served bourbon since bourbon and bars met."

Sidecar Named Desire

This drink was the 2013 Grand Champion at the Kentucky Bourbon Festival Mixed Drink Challenge. We developed it here at our bourbon bar.

Submitted by: Old Talbott

Serve in a highball glass:
- 1 ½ ounces Woodford Reserve Bourbon
- 1 ½ ounces strawberry simple syrup
- 1 ½ ounces apple cider
- ½ ounce lemon juice
- ½ ounce Cointreau
- Serve in a martini glass with strawberry garnish

Strawberry Simple Syrup
- 2 pounds strawberries
- 2 cups sugar
- 1 quart water
- Rinse, hull and slice strawberries
- Put strawberries in a medium sauce pan and cover with water
- Light boil for 20 minutes
- Skim the foam off top
- Remove from heat and strain
- Do not press strawberries as it will make the finished product cloudy
- Return strawberry liquid to pan and bring to a boil
- Add sugar and stir until dissolved
- Boil an additional 5 minutes
- Put in container (bottle with pourer)

The Tavern In Old Salem

736 South Main Street
Winston-Salem, NC 27101
(336) 722-1227

thetaverninoldsalem.ws
info@thetaverninoldsalem.com

Established
1784

Leadership
The Keiper Family

The Keiper family (mother, father and three sons) purchased this historic restaurant and tavern in 2012. Son Jordan is quickly becoming a noted mixologist having created over 800 unique cocktails in 2014. Jordan has plans for his own book, but in the meantime, his submission here is clearing hurdles to attempt to win the distinction of ***Restaurant Hospitality Magazine's*** "Best Cocktail in America."

The Bourbon Berry Smash

Inspired by Eastern culture meets Western culture, the challenge was to create a refreshing whiskey-based cocktail using Japanese sake and plum wines. A fun drink to create, you will definitely impress your guests with this creative drink.

Submitted by: Jordan Keiper, Co-Owner and Mixologist

Serve in a rocks glass:
- 1 ½ ounce bourbon
- 4 blackberries
- 12 blueberries
- 1 ounce Gekkeikan Plum Wine
- ¼ ounce Madagascar vanilla bean simple syrup (recipe below)
- 1 ounce Bittermilk no.3 Smoked Honey Whiskey Sour
- 2 dashes Scrappy's Aromatic Bitters
- Muddle fresh blackberries and blueberries in shaker until all are crushed well
- Add 1 ½ ounce bourbon, plum vine, vanilla bean simple syrup, smoked honey whiskey sour and bitters to shaker
- Add ice and shake well to combine ingredient's
- Strain over ice in a rocks glass and garnish with additional blueberries and blackberries

Vanilla Simple Syrup
- 8 ounces water
- 8 ounces sugar
- 2 ounces Madagascar vanilla extract
- In a small pot combine water sugar and extract and bring to boil

Vanilla Simple Syrup *(continued)*
- Simmer mixture for five minutes
- Let cool in refrigerator and serve

Tonga Hut Palm Springs

254 N. Palm Canyon Drive
Palm Springs, CA 92262
(336) 722-1227

tongahut.com
amy@tongahut.com

Established
2013/Palm Springs location (original location opened in 1958)

Leadership
Amy Boylan, Managing Partner
Stephanie Nolet, Manager

The original Tonga Hut (12808 Victory Boulevard, North Hollywood, CA 91606) is a neighborhood bar that holds the distinction of being L.A.'s oldest Tiki bar still in operation. The Tonga Hut first opened its doors in 1958 by brothers Ace & Ed Libby. Today, much of the original decor still remains, including pecky cedar walls, a kidney-shaped drop ceiling, fountains, and tikis. Enter the dimly-lit Tonga Hut, settle into a booth or sidle up to the bar and enjoy an exotic cocktail that will bring you back to an era long gone.

Tiki My Bourbon

In 2013, Tonga Hut expanded opening a Tonga Hut Bar and Restaurant in Palm Springs, California. Tonga Palm Springs carries on the legacy with the same tiki modern style and laid back atmospheres and Tonga Hut PS serves up the same great drinks using fresh ingredients as the original Tonga Hut.

Submitted by: Stephanie Nolet

Serve in a rocks glass:
- 2 ½ ounces Makers Mark Bourbon
- 1 ounce fresh or unsweetened coconut water
- 1 ounce pineapple juice
- 2 dashes Fees Peach Bitters
- ½ ounce hibiscus simple syrup
- In a 9 ounce rocks glass, pour hibiscus simple syrup
- In a shaker, pour all other ingredients
- Shake and pour over hibiscus simple syrup
- Garnish with pineapple leaves and orchid

The West End Tavern

96 Pearl Street
Boulder, CO 80302
(303) 444-3535

thewestendtavern.com
info@thewestendtavern.com

Established
1987

Leadership
Dave Query, Owner

Go Fig or Go Home

Submitted by: Jackie Dunlap

Serve in a rocks glass:
- 2 ounces fig-infused bourbon (Suggested: Four Roses Bourbon/yellow label)
- ¼ ounce orange simple syrup
- The juice of one squeezed lemon
- 2 dashes black walnut bitters
- Combine ingredients into rocks glass, stir on ice
- Strain into fresh ice in an Absinthe rinsed rocks glass
- Garnish with candied orange peel

Candied Orange Peel Recipe
- 4 large oranges
- 8 cups of sugar
- 6 cups of water
- Cut orange peels into equal vertical segments and then cut into ¼ inch strips
- Cook orange peels in boiling water for 15 minutes, drain and rinse
- Bring 6 cups water and 6 cups sugar to a boil and stir to dissolve sugar
- Add orange peels and return to a boil, reduce heat and simmer for 45 minutes
- Place peels on baking sheet and coat the peels with 2 cups sugar
- Transfer peels to clean baking sheet or foil and let cool until coating is dry

Whiskey Bar

788 N. Jackson Street
Milwaukee, WI 53202

whiskeybarmilwaukee.com

Leadership
Ben Richardson, General Manager

Cathedral Square Cocktail

Submitted by: Ben Richardson, General Manager

Serve in a collins glass:
- 1 ¼ ounces Bulleit Bourbon
- ¼ ounce Amaro Nonino
- ⅓ ounce Chartreuse
- 3 dashes of Fee Brothers Grapefruit Bitters
- ½ ounce fresh lemon juice
- ½ ounce rosemary simple syrup
- Garnish with a sprig of rosemary & lemon wedge

Whiskey Kitchen

118 12th Avenue South
Nashville, TN 37203
(615) 254-3029

whiskeykitchen.com

Established
2009

Leadership
MStreet Entertainment Group

The New Fashioned
Whiskey Kitchen's spin on an "old" favorite.

Submitted by: Whiskey Kitchen

Serve in a rocks glass:
- 2 ounces Old Forester Bourbon
- Spoonful of diced apple
- Spoonful of brandied cherries
- Dash of cinnamon
- 2 dashes old fashioned bitters
- ½ ounce simple syrup
- Mix all ingredients together in a rocks glass and stir

Windmill Lounge

5320 Maple Avenue
Dallas, TX 75235
(502) 473-8560

windmill-lounge.com
windmilllounge@gmail.com

Established
2005

Sensuous Summer Sipper

This cocktail was inspired by memories of hot summer days in NYC in the 1980s and the joy of an ice cold Manhattan Special Soda from the deli or an egg cream at Bigelow's Pharmacy on 6th Avenue when they still had the lunch counter. Toss in a yearning for an Austrian Eiskaffee made with dark roast coffee and vanilla ice cream topped off with whipped cream and we created the Sensuous Summer Sipper.

Submitted by: Louise Owens, The Windmill Lounge

Serve in a large stemless wine glass:

- 1 ½ ounces bourbon
- 1 ounce espresso syrup (see below)
- A very healthy dollop of whipped cream, unsweetened if at all possible
- Seltzer
- Combine bourbon, espresso syrup and whipped cream in a cocktail shaker
- *DRY* shake until all ingredients are combined
- Pour into the wineglass
- Top off with 2-3 ounces of seltzer and add ice
- This will create a two-tiered drink with a coffee/bourbon froth on the top and a base of sweet deliciousness

Espresso Syrup Recipe

- 16 ounces strong Italian or French roast coffee
- 16 ounces sugar
- Combine in a saucepan and a simmer until the mixture begins to thicken to a syrup
- Remove from heat and allow to cool

Wiseguy Lounge at Goodfellas Pizzeria

603 Main Street
Covington, KY 41011
(859) 516-5209
Check Website for more locations

goodfellaspizzeria.com
goodfellaspizzeria@gmail.com

Established
2012

Leadership
Alex Coats, Co-Owner
Eric Boggs, Co-Owner
Bill Whitlow, Beverage Director

Wiseguy Lounge is a speakeasy located upstairs from Goodfellas Pizzeria. You have to go through the pizzeria and up a back stairwell to get to the bar.

The Bossman-Hattan

This cocktail was one of the first created for Wiseguy Lounge. It was conceived to be a slightly sweeter take on a bourbon Manhattan, with a nicely rounded out profile. We named it as an ode to Al Capone, as he was the Bossman during prohibition. It has since become the house favorite and remains on our cocktail menu at all times.

Submitted by: Bill Whitlow

Serve in a coupe:
- 1 ½ ounces Old Forester Signature Bourbon
- ½ ounce Dolin Sweet Vermouth
- ½ ounce Dumante Pistachio Liqueur
- 1 bar spoon vanilla syrup
- 3 dashes Fee Brothers Rhubarb Bitters
- Add all ingredients to a glass and add ice
- Stir for about 10 seconds
- Strain into a coupe with a brandied cherry garnish

Index of Cocktails by Name

Author's Notes/Resources

I encourage you to learn more about these businesses and what makes them so special. To make your job a little easier, here's a recap of the websites for each:

Bale of Hay Saloon – *baleofhaysaloon.com*

Big Star – *bigstarchicago.com*

Bourbons Bistro – *bourbonsbistro.com*

Bourbon and Branch – *bourbonandbranch.com*

Bourbon House – *bourbonhouse.com*

Bub City – *bubcitychicago.com*

Buckhorn Exchange – *buckhorn.com*

Buffalo Bodega Gaming Complex – *buffalobodega.com*

Butter Run Saloon – *butterrun.com*

Down One Bourbon Bar and Restaurant – *downonebourbonbar.com*

E. Smith Mercantile – *esmithmercantile.com*

El Gaucho – *elgaucho.com*

El Moro Spirits & Tavern – *elmorotavern.com*

Equus and Jack's Lounge – *equusrestaurant.com*

The Esquire Tavern – *esquiretavern-sa.com*

FAR BAR – *farbarla.com*

Forbidden Island Tiki Lounge – *forbiddenislandalameda.com*

Gallagher's Restaurant – *gallagherswaterloo.com*

Hard Water – *hardwaterbar.com*

Herbie's Vintage 72 – *herbies.com*

Jack Rose Dining Saloon – *jackrosediningsaloon.com*

The Lovecraft Bar – *lovecraftbar.com*

Martin's Tavern – *martinstavern.com*

Mike Shannon's Steaks and Seafood – *shannonsteak.com*

The Miller House – *themillerhouserestaurant.com*

Mongoose versus Cobra - *mongooseversuscobra.com*

9th Street Public House – *9thstreetpublichouse.com*

Old Ebbitt Grill – *ebbitt.com*

Old Major – *oldmajor.com*

Parlay Social – *parlaysocial.com*

Parson's Chicken and Fish – *parsonschickenandfish.com*

Peacock Alley – *peacocock-alley.com*

The Pope House Bourbon Lounge – *popehouselounge.com*

The Porthole Restaurant and Pub – *portholemaine.com*

Red Moon – *redmoonbar.com*

The Roosevelt – *rooseveltrva.com*

Round Robin at The Williard – *washington.intercontinental.com*

Sable Kitchen & Bar – *sablechicago.com*

Sanctuaria Wild Tapas – *sanctuariastl.com*

Seviche, A Latin Restaurant – *sevicherestaurant.com*

Sloppy Joe's – *sloppyjoes.com*

Snow and Co. – *snowandcompany.com*

St. Charles Exchange – *stcharlesexchange.com*

The Sugar House – *sugarhousedetroit.com*

Talbott Tavern – *talbotts.com*

The Tavern In Old Salem – *thetaverninoldsalem.ws*

Tonga Hut – *tongahut.com*

The West End Tavern – *thewestendtavern.com*

Whiskey Bar – *whiskeybarmilwaukee.com*

Whiskey Kitchen – *whiskeykitchen.com*

Windmill Lounge – *windmill-lounge.com*

Wiseguy Lounge – *goodfellaspizzeria.com*

Small Brand America V
Special Bourbon Edition

In ***Small Brand America V***, author Steve Akley explores small companies making a name for themselves with a truly American original: bourbon. Each has a little bit of a different take on making America's favorite distilled spirit and a compelling story. Inevitably, you will find yourself wanting to learn more about the companies and a desire to try their product(s).

Pa'u Hana

Pa'u Hana, the story of two friends living in Hawai'i looking to break into the movie business is Steve Akley's first novel. Steve delivers a hilarious buddy story about the greatest adventure of these two best friends' lives.

The Importance of Online Reviews

⭐⭐⭐⭐⭐ I love it

Write your review here

⭐⭐⭐⭐☆ I like it

Write your review here

⭐⭐⭐☆☆ It's okay

Write your review here

⭐⭐☆☆☆ I don't like it

Write your review here

⭐☆☆☆☆ I hate it

Write your review here

Reviews generate interest and create a buzz about the work of an author. Plus, your feedback is the only way an author knows if you enjoyed their work. Please take the time to review *Bourbon Mixology*! Steve would love to know what you think!

Photo Credits

All photographs in the sections of each business featured have been utilized with permission from the respective companies with the following exceptions:

Bub City
Anjali Pinto – Bub City cocktail

E. Smith Mercantile
Belathee Photography – E. Smith Mercantile bar

Old Ebbitt Grill
Clyde's Restaurant Group – Old Ebbitt Grill bar
Clyde's Restaurant Group – Michter's Manhattan cocktail

The Roosevelt
John Murden – Providence and Grace cocktail and building

Sancturia Wild Tapas
Daniel Parker – Clermont Confusion cocktail

Seviche, A Latin Restaurant
Jolea Brown – Outdoor view of Seviche

Sloppy Joe's
Rob O'Neal – Sloppy Joe's bar

Special Thanks

To my mom, Sandy Akley, and my wife Amy Akley, my sister-in-law Lee Ann Sciuto and my friend Mary Banta-Schmitt for their help in editing this book.

Thanks to my daughter Cat for just being herself.

Hats off to Mark Hansen (*mappersmark@gmail.com*) for the great cover design. He's the greatest graphic artist you will ever find!

The following individuals from the featured companies not only couldn't have been nicer, without their help this book would not have been possible:
Heather and Gay Rossow/Bale of Hay Saloon, Wesley Noble, Whitney Guarisco and Barry Himel/Bourbon House, Charlie Schott/Parson's Chicken and Fish, Donna Edwards/Sloppy Joe's, Dale Zimmerman/Peacock Alley, Lauren Farrar and Colin Shearn/St. Charles Exchange, Michael Thanos/Forbidden Island Tiki Lounge, Christopher Murray/Buckhorn Exchange, Larry Kirk/The Miller House, Jennifer Liberman/oneoffhospitality.com, Laurent Lebec/Big Star, Amanda Clephas Lambert/Al J. Schneider Company, Beth Burrows/Down One Bourbon Bar, Chris Derome/Seviche, Madeline Doolittle/Seviche, Laura Meyers/Bullfrog + Baum, Diane Corcora/Bub City, Sarah Feinauer/Whiskey Bar, Ben Richardson/Whiskey Bar, Beth Silverberg/El Gaucho Hospitality Group, by James Capangpangan/El Gaucho, Daniel Parker/Sanctuaria Wild Tapas, Sonny Geha/Butter Run Saloon, Jordan Keiper/The Tavern in Old Salem, Brook Moreno/Lovecraft Bar, Jon Horrid/Lovecraft Bar, Kate, Jesse and Sara Poole/E. Smith Mercantile, Michelle Banovic/Kimpton Hotels & Restaurants, Justin Brunson/Old Major, Mike McGill/Old Major, Erik Adkins/Slanted Door Group, Jennifer Colliau/Small Hand Foods, Aaron Teitelbaum/Herbie's Vintage 72, Amanda Wilgus/Herbie's Vintage 72, Anthony Hesselius/Linda Roth Associates, Jim Hewes/Round Robin, Rob Lyons/Buffalo Bodega Gaming Complex, Houston Eaves/The Esquire Tavern, Myles Worrell/The Esquire Tavern, Beth Poitras/The Porthole Restaurant and Pub, Andrew MacDonald/The Porthole Restaurant and Pub, Tricia Shannon/Mike Shannon's Steaks and Seafood,

Chrissy Gardner/Martin's Tavern, Thomas Leggett/The Roosevelt, Katy Adams/Clyde's Restaurant Group, Ian Rosenberg/Mongoose vs. Cobra, Joel Carson/The Pope House Bourbon Lounge, Miles Kusch/The Pope House Bourbon Lounge, Louise Owens/Windmill Lounge, Jim/Talbott Tavern, Jordan Keiper/The Tavern In Old Salem, Jason Leinart/The Sugar House, Bob Estes/Parlay Social, Michael De Leon/9th Street Public House, James Gallagher/Gallagher's Restaurant, Stephanie Nolet/Tonga Hut, Amy Boylan/Tonga Hut, Dave Woodruff/El Moro Spirits & Tavern, Brittany Garrison/ThreeLockharts Public Relations, Bill Whitlow/Wiseguy Lounge, Paula Garsteck/Red Moon, Ciara Flaherty/Future Bars, Ann Harlow/Bourbons Bistro, Jerry Nevins/Snow and Co., Jackie Berkley/MStreet Entertainment Group, Ryan Arnett/Equus and Jack's Lounge and Joy Perrine/Equus and Jack's Lounge, Sean Naughton/FAR BAR, Mike Gin/FAR BAR and Chelsea Wickens/West End Tavern.

It wasn't just me tracking down the iconic bars you have read about in this book. The following friends and family also helped by sharing some of their favorite places:
Charlie and Sue Robertson, Laura Roth, Mary Banta-Schmitt, Annie Porn, Chris Sciuto, Tyler Shepard, Jeff Rowlee, Ginnie Blaine, Holly Stahlman, Megan Blaufuss and Bob Scavina.

Lastly, lots of love for my father, Larry Akley. He's always with us in spirit.

In Loving Memory of Larry Akley
1942 – 2012

About the Author

Steve Akley is a lifelong St. Louis resident. Steve's approach to his writing is very simple. He knows his passion for writing comes from topics he enjoys so he sticks to what he knows best.

And yes... he likes bourbon:

Sign up for his newsletter, or check out his latest work, on his website: steveakley.com. Steve also maintains an author's page on Amazon.com. Just search his name on the site.

He can be reached via email: info@steveakley.com.

Find Steve on Social Media

 @steveakley WORDPRESS & Steve Akley

Also by Steve Akley

Leo the Coffee Drinking Cat Series

A children's series featuring the adventures of a coffee drinking cat named Leo and his family.

Coffeehouse Jazz

Designed to assist you in building the ultimate playlists of jazz music. At 99¢, they cost less than the price of downloading a single song!

Steve Akley's Commuter Series

Short stories available for Kindle, iBooks and other electronic retailers

Only $1.49 each!

Be sure to check out Steve's website:

www.steveakley.com